A Pet's Life

Cats

Anita Ganeri

Heinemann
LIBRARY

www.heinemannlibrary.co.uk

Visit our website to find out more information about Heinemann Library books.

To order:

☎ Phone +44 (0) 1865 888066

🖷 Fax +44 (0) 1865 314091

🖳 Visit www.heinemannlibrary.co.uk

Heinemann Library is an imprint of Capstone Global Library Limited, a company incorporated in England and Wales having its registered office at 7 Pilgrim Street, London, EC4V 6LB – Registered company number: 6695582

"Heinemann" is a registered trademark of Pearson Education Limited, under licence to Capstone Global Library Limited.

Edited by Charlotte Guillain and Harriet Milles
Designed by Joanna Hinton-Malivoire
Picture research by Elizabeth Alexander and Rebecca Sodergren
Production by Victoria Fitzgerald
Originated by Chroma Graphics (Overseas) Pte. Ltd
Printed and bound in China by South China Printing Company Ltd.

ISBN 978 0 4311 7787 8 (hardback)
13 12 11 10 09
10 9 8 7 6 5 4 3 2 1

ISBN 978 0 4311 7794 6 (paperback)
13 12 11 10 09
10 9 8 7 6 5 4 3 2

British Library Cataloguing in Publication Data
Ganeri, Anita, 1961-
   Cats. - 2nd ed. - (A pet's life)
   1. Cats - Juvenile literature
   I. Title
   636.8
A full catalogue record for this book is available from the British Library.

Acknowledgements

We would like to thank the following for permission to reproduce photographs:
Alamy pp. **15** (© Juniors Bildarchiv), **16** (© isobel flynn); Ardea pp. **4**, **18**, **19** (John Daniels); © Capstone Global Library Ltd. pp. **12**, **17**, **25** (Tudor Photography); Corbis p. **27** (© David Shopper); Dorling Kindersley pp. **10** (Daniel Pangbourne), **14** (Jane Burton); Getty Images p. **21** (Steve Lyne); NaturePL.com p. **24** (© Jane Burton); RSPCA pp. **8** (Andrew Forsyth), **23**, **26** (Angela Hampton); Warren Photographic pp. **5**, **6**, **7**, **9**, **11**, **13**, **20**, **22** (Jane Burton).

Cover photograph of a tabby cat reproduced with permission of Shutterstock (© mares).

The publishers would like to thank Rob Lee for his assistance in the preparation of this book.

Every effort has been made to contact copyright holders of material reproduced in this book. Any omissions will be rectified in subsequent printings if notice is given to the publishers.

Contents

Any words appearing in the text in bold, **like this**, are explained in the Glossary.

What do cats look like?

There are many kinds of pet cats. Cats can be big or small. They can have long, fluffy hair, or short hair. Cats are very popular pets.

This cat has long, fluffy hair.

This picture shows the different parts of a cat's body. You can see what each part is used for.

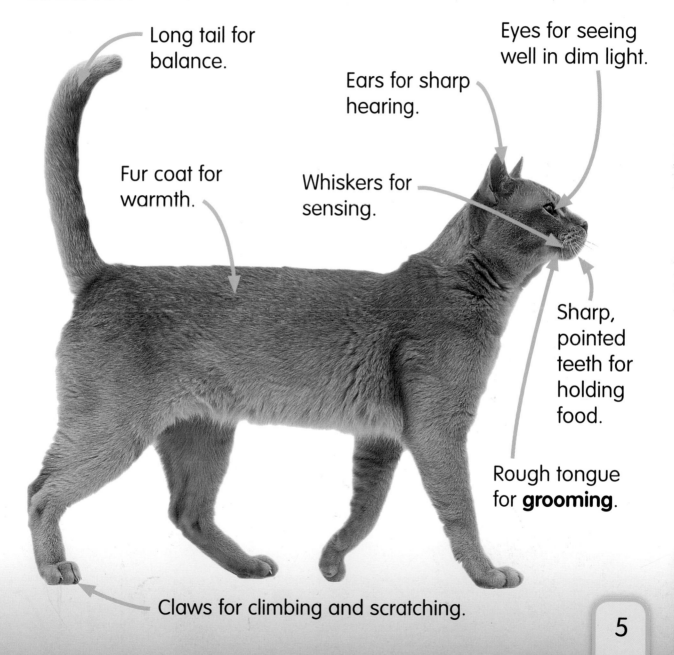

Long tail for balance.

Eyes for seeing well in dim light.

Ears for sharp hearing.

Fur coat for warmth.

Whiskers for sensing.

Sharp, pointed teeth for holding food.

Rough tongue for **grooming**.

Claws for climbing and scratching.

Cat babies

Baby cats are called kittens. A new-born kitten is small and helpless. Its mother licks it to keep it clean. The kitten opens its eyes when it is about five to ten days old.

New-born kittens feed on their mother's milk.

Kittens love to play with their brothers and sisters.

Kittens must be about eight weeks old
before they can leave their mother.
Then they are ready to be chosen as pets.

Choosing your cat

The best place to find a cat or kitten is an **animal shelter**. They are always looking for good homes for cats of all kinds and ages.

You may decide to get an adult cat instead of a kitten.

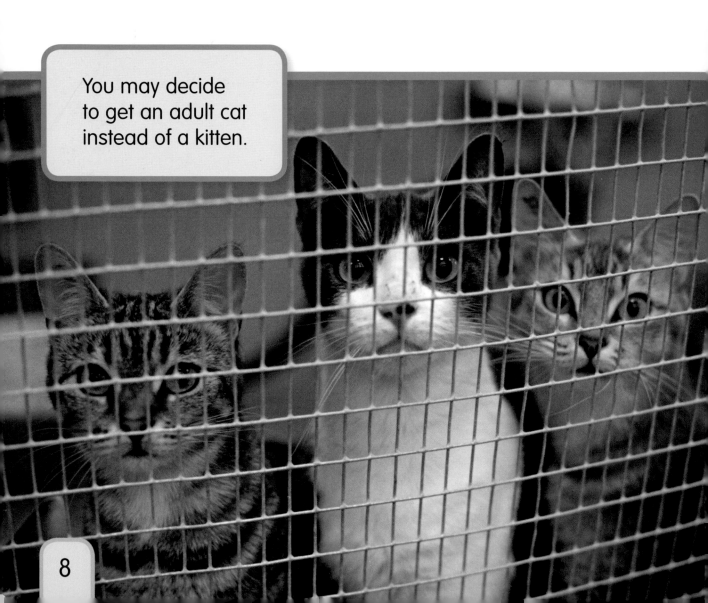

Look for a friendly, lively kitten that likes to play.

Pick a cat or kitten with bright eyes, clean ears, and a clean nose. Check that its coat is shiny and that its bottom is dry and clean.

Things to get ready

Get everything ready before you bring your new pet home. Your cat will need a cosy basket or bed to sleep in. It will need bowls for food and water.

Put your cat's bed in a clean, quiet place.

Clean the litter tray every day. Don't forget to wash your hands afterwards.

Your cat will also need a plastic **litter tray** where it can go to the toilet. You can buy a tray, and bags of litter, from a pet shop.

Welcome home

You can carry your cat home in a special carrying box made from wire and plastic, or cardboard. Line the box with newspaper and a warm blanket or towel.

A carrying box is also useful for taking your cat to the **vet**.

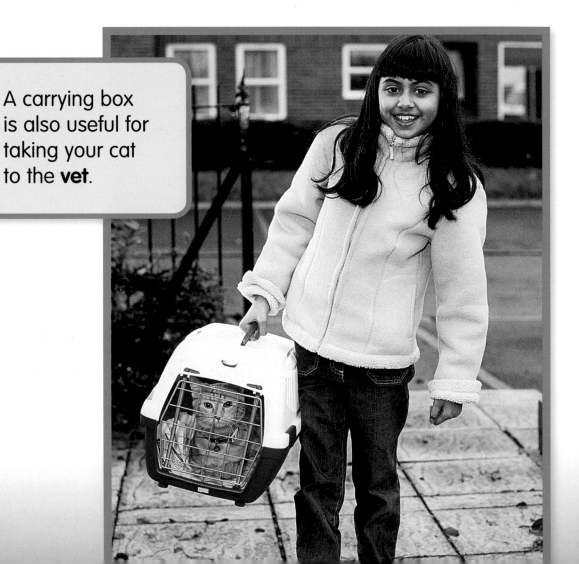

If you have another pet, let your new cat get to know it slowly.

For a few days, leave your new pet in one room to help it settle in quietly. Then you can let it explore the whole house.

Feeding time

You can feed your cat on dry or tinned food. Adult cats need two meals a day. Kittens should have three to four smaller meals.

Kittens should have special kitten food to help them grow.

Wash your cat's food and water bowls every day.

Make sure that your cat always has clean water to drink. It is not a good idea to give your cat milk. Milk might make your cat ill.

Training your cat

Kittens have to be trained to use a **litter tray**. Start by lifting your kitten gently into its tray. Do this often until it learns to use the tray on its own.

Your kitten will soon learn to use the litter tray on its own.

Your cat will quickly learn to push a cat-flap open with its head.

Most cats like to go outside. Fit a **cat-flap** into your door. At first, you can prop it open to let your cat go in and out.

Playing with your cat

Kittens love to play. You can buy special cat toys from a pet shop. Cardboard tubes, cotton reels, and paper bags also make good toys.

Playing will teach your kitten new skills.

Your cat has to scratch with its claws to keep them sharp. Outdoors, cats can scratch trees. A cat's scratching post is good for indoors.

A cat's scratching post is covered with carpet or rope.

Growing up

Kittens grow up very quickly. By the time they are a year old, they are adult cats. Male cats usually grow bigger than female cats.

The cat on the left is male. You can see that he is bigger than the female.

As it gets older, your cat will still like to play.

There are a great many unwanted cats and kittens. It is best to have your kitten or cat **neutered** to stop it having babies. Ask your **vet** about this.

A healthy cat

You need to look after your cat to make sure that it stays healthy. If you are worried about your cat, take it to a **vet**.

If your cat stops eating or drinking, it may be unwell.

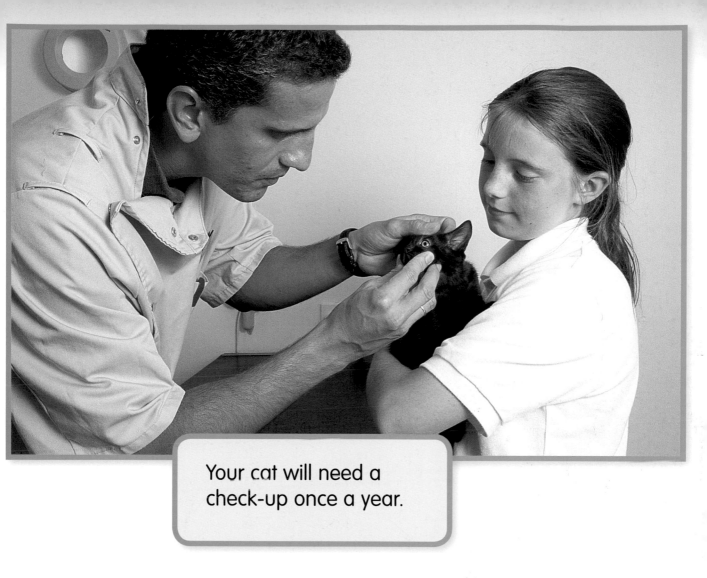

Your cat will need a check-up once a year.

When you get a new cat or kitten, take it to the vet for a check-up. When your kitten is nine weeks old, the vet will give it **injections** to stop it getting ill.

Your pet cat

Looking after a cat is fun but it also takes lots of time. You need to look after your cat every day, for the whole of its life.

If you look after your cat, it will quickly become your best friend.

If you go on holiday, ask a friend or a neighbour to look after your cat. Otherwise you can put your cat in a **cattery**.

Make a list of what your friend needs to do for your cat.

Old age

Cats can live for a long time, usually for about 12 to 16 years. As your cat gets older, it might need special care.

As it gets older, your cat will want to sleep more.

Older cats cannot see or hear as well as young cats. Jumping becomes hard, too. But your cat will still liked to be held and cuddled.

Caring for your cat will help you learn how to treat animals properly.

Useful tips

- The **vet** can fit your cat with a **microchip** so that it can be easily found if it gets lost. Otherwise, your cat should wear a collar and tag with your name and address on it. Choose a collar that will snap open if it gets caught on something.

- Cats are very clean and **groom** themselves with their tongues. But long-haired cats need to be brushed every day. This will stop them from swallowing too much fur and getting **fur balls**.

- Ask your vet what medicines you should give your cat to stop it getting fleas and worms.

- Look at the label on the cat food to find out how much to give to your cat. Do not give your cat too much to eat.

Fact file

- Cats were first kept as pets about 4,000 years ago. They were used to catch mice and rats.

- Cats were popular pets in ancient Egypt. People thought they were gods who could do magic.

- Cats can sleep for 16 to 18 hours a day.

- The oldest pet cat known was called Crème Puff. It live to be 38 years old. It died in 2005.

- Your pet cat's wild relatives include lions, tigers, leopards, and cheetahs.

- Most cats have 18 toes. Cats with 20 or more toes are called "polydactyl" cats.

Glossary

animal shelter place where lost or unwanted animals are looked after

cat-flap flap that you fit in a door to let your cat go in and out

cattery place where you can leave your cat when you go on holiday

fur ball ball of fur that a cat has swallowed

groom gently brush your cat's fur. Cats also groom themselves using their rough tongues.

injection medicine that is given by a vet to stop your cat catching diseases

litter tray box where a cat can go to the toilet. It is filled with special gravel called litter.

microchip tiny tag with a special number on it to help you find your cat if it gets lost

neutered when a cat has an operation so that it cannot have any babies

vet specially trained animal doctor

More information

Books to read

First Pets: Cats and Kittens, K. Starke (Usborne Publishing, 2nd ed., 2004)

How to Look After Your Pet: Kitten, Mark Evans (Dorling Kindersley, 1992)

RSPCA Pet Guide: Care for your Cat (Collins, 2004)

RSPCA Pet Guide: Care for your Kitten (Collins, 2004)

Websites

www.rspca.org.uk
The website of The Royal Society for the Prevention of Cruelty to Animals in Britain.

www.pethealthcare.co.uk
Information about caring for first pets.

www.petlink.com.au
Information about being a good pet owner.

Index